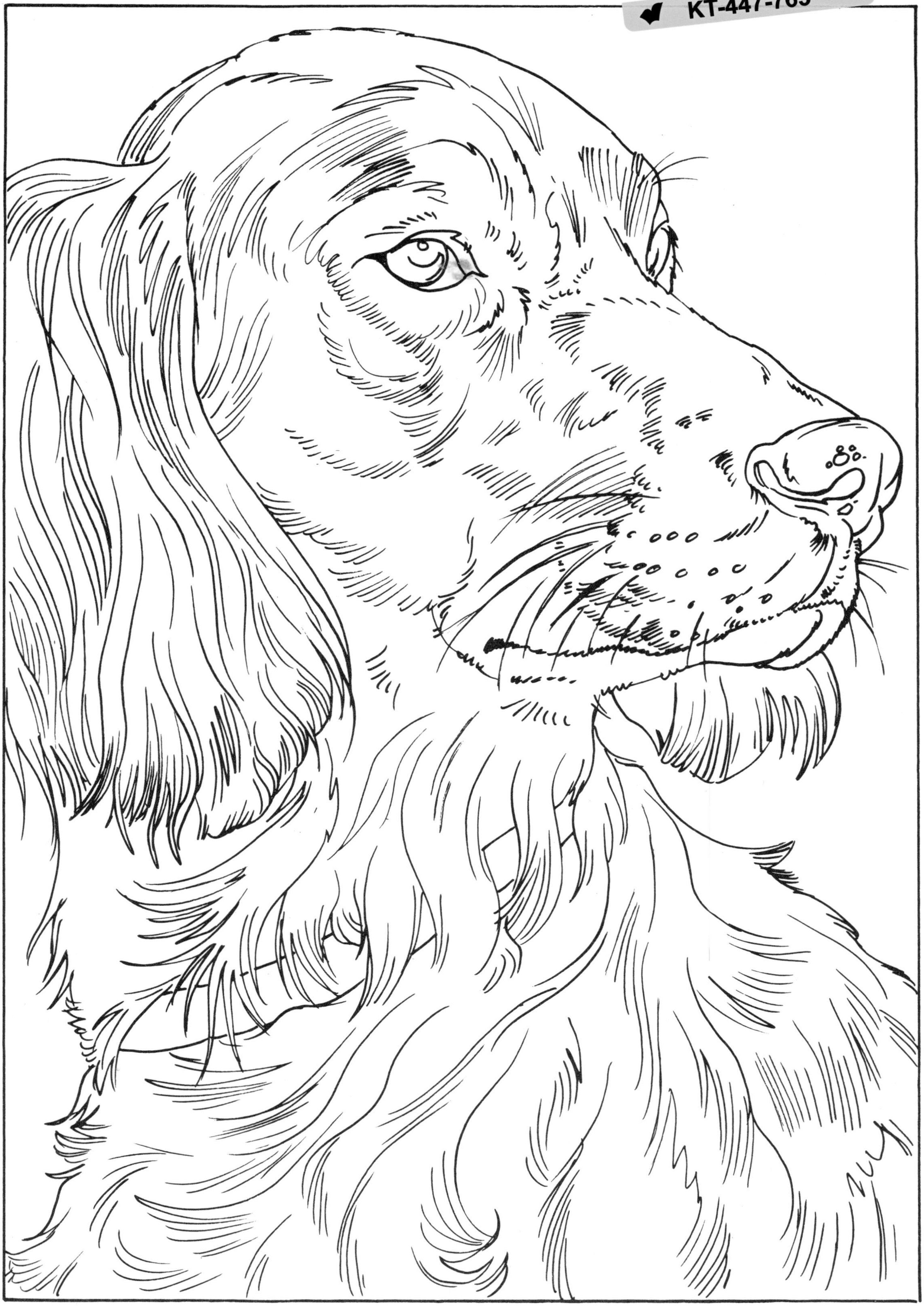

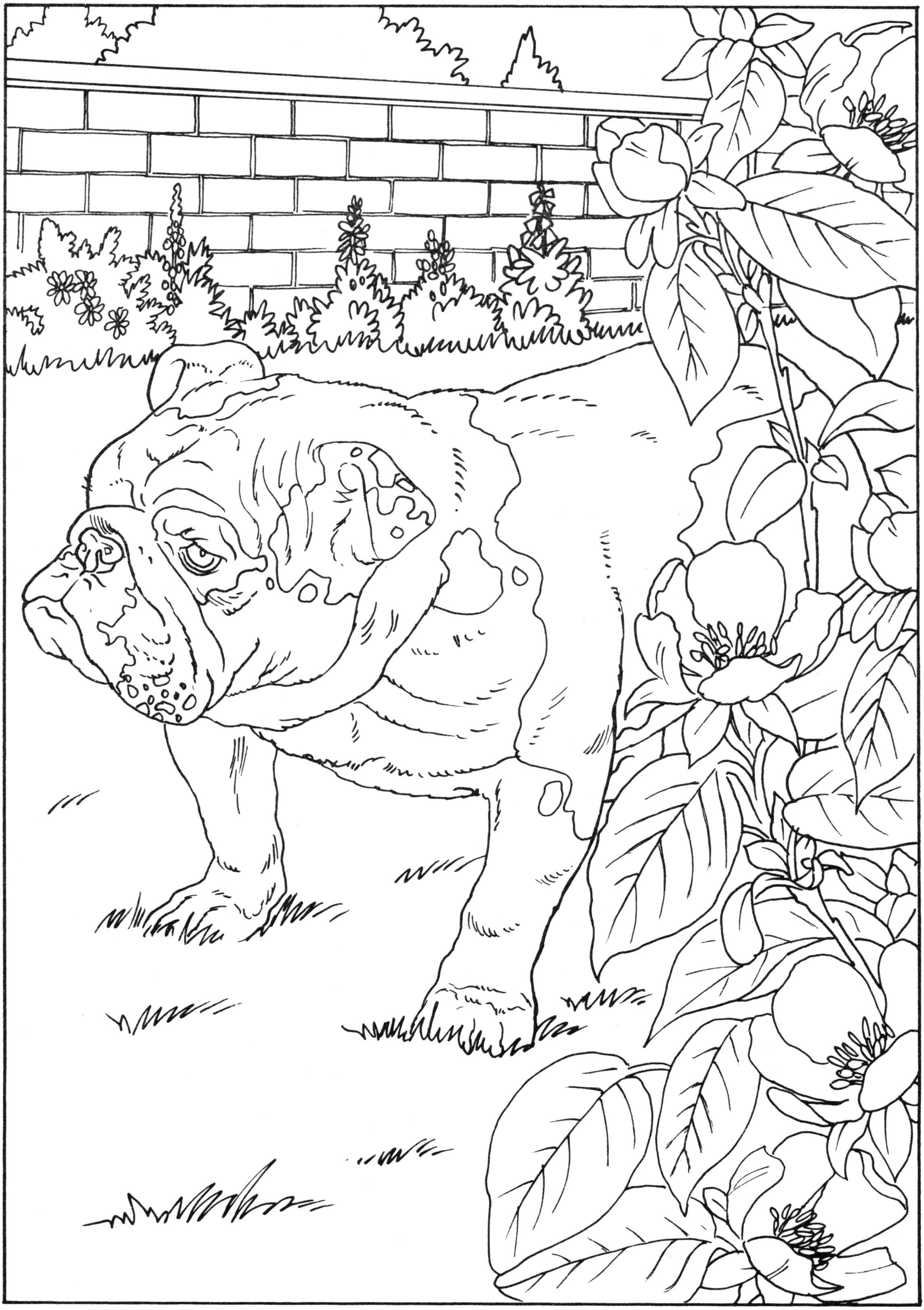

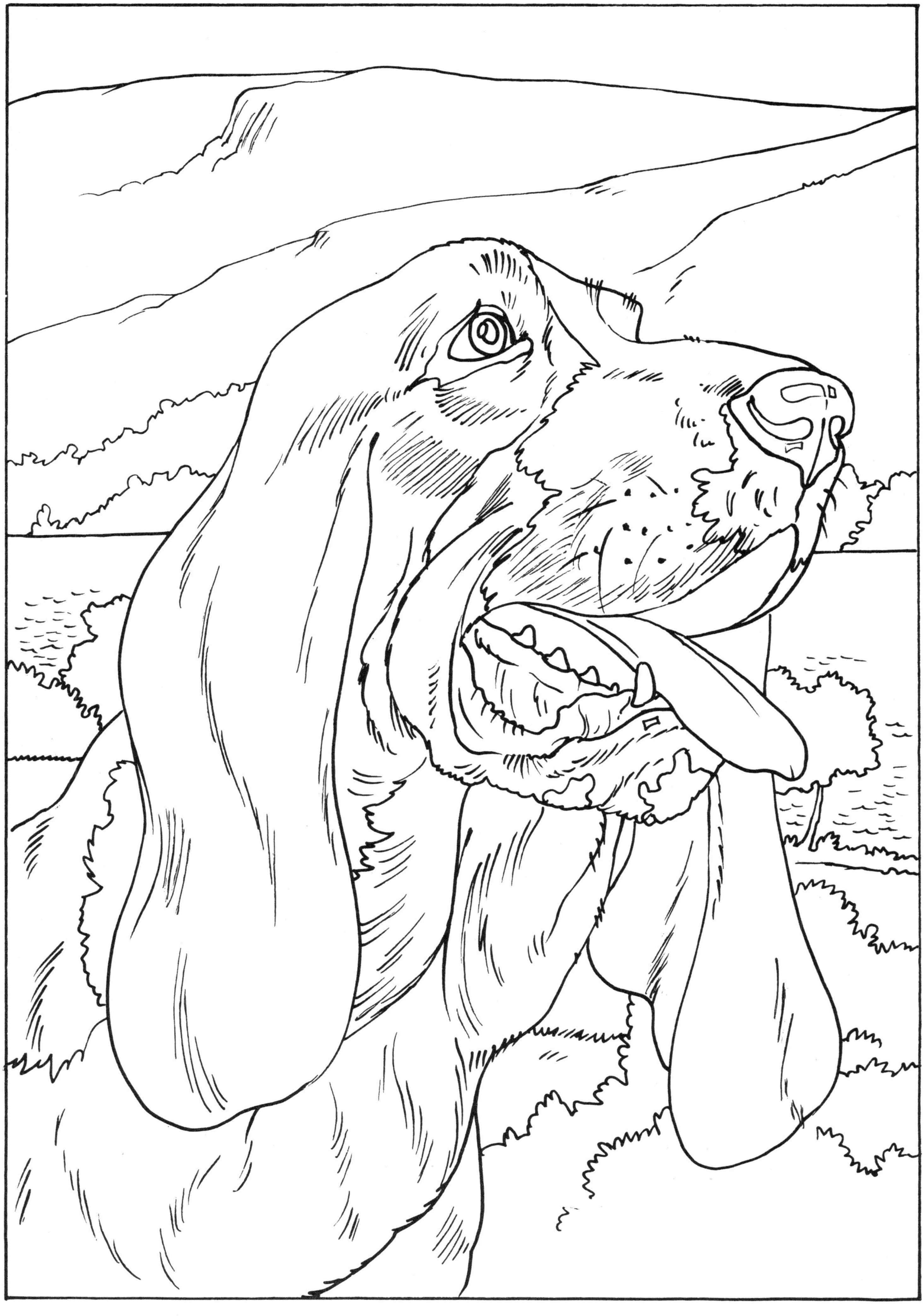

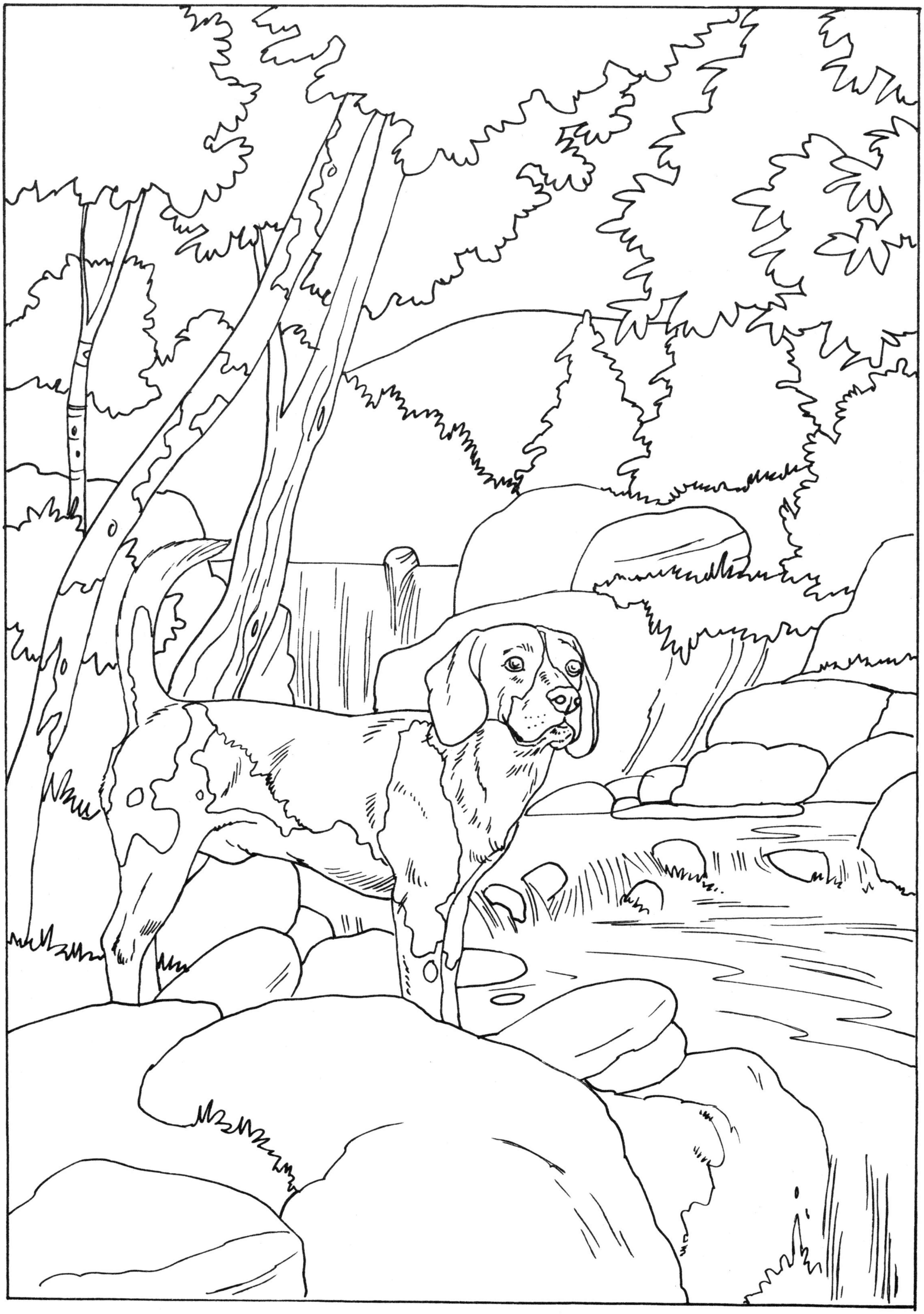

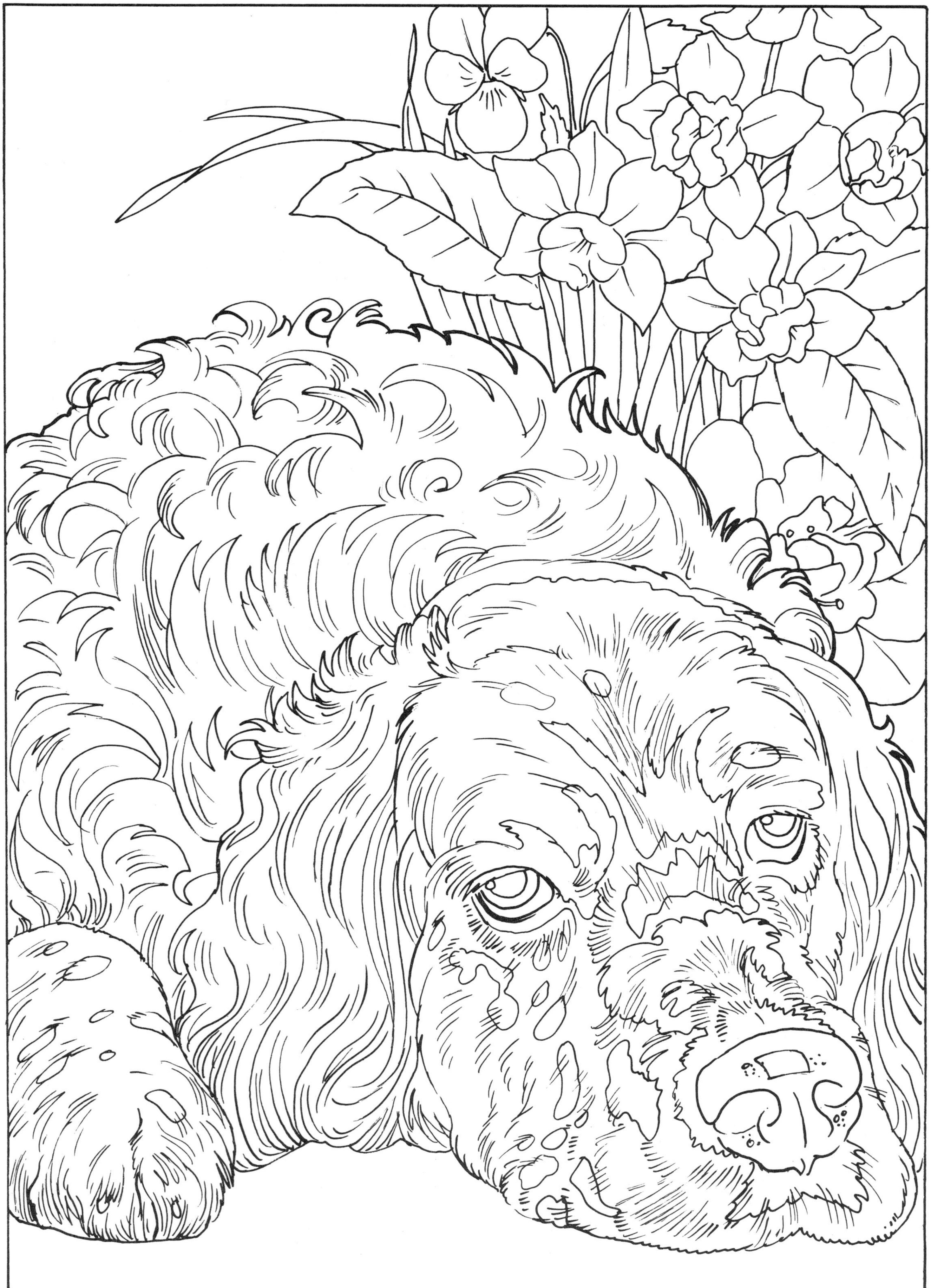

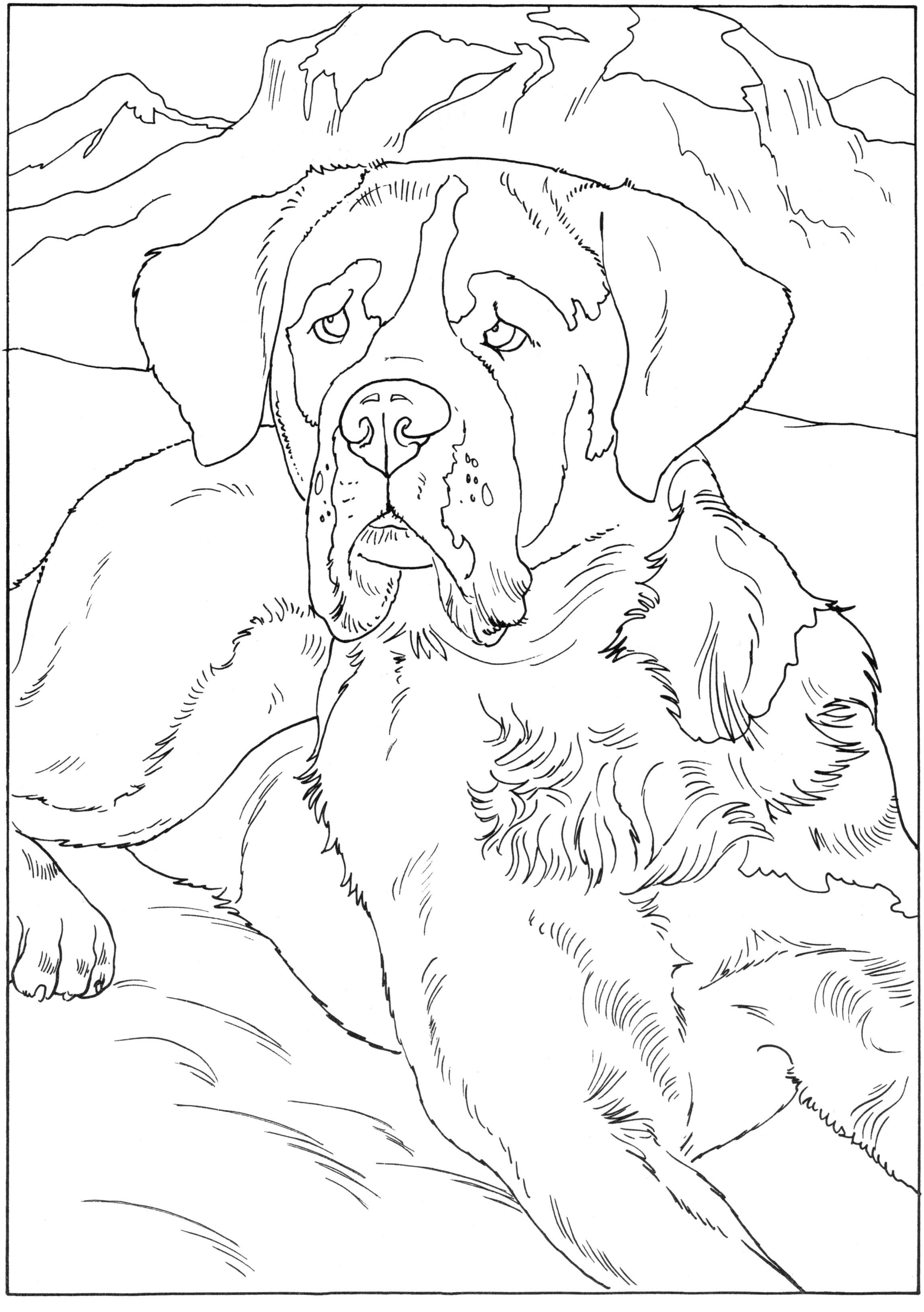

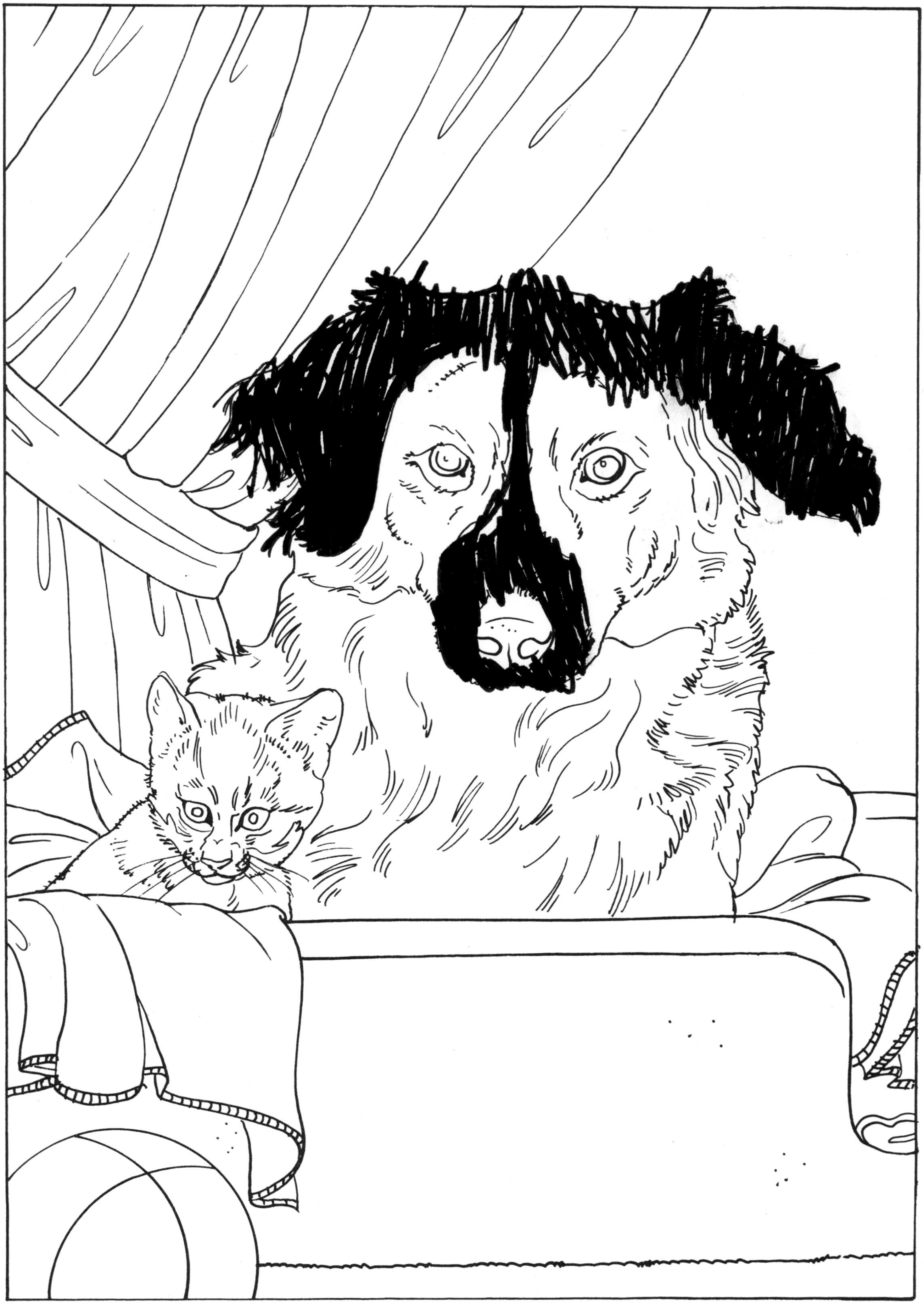

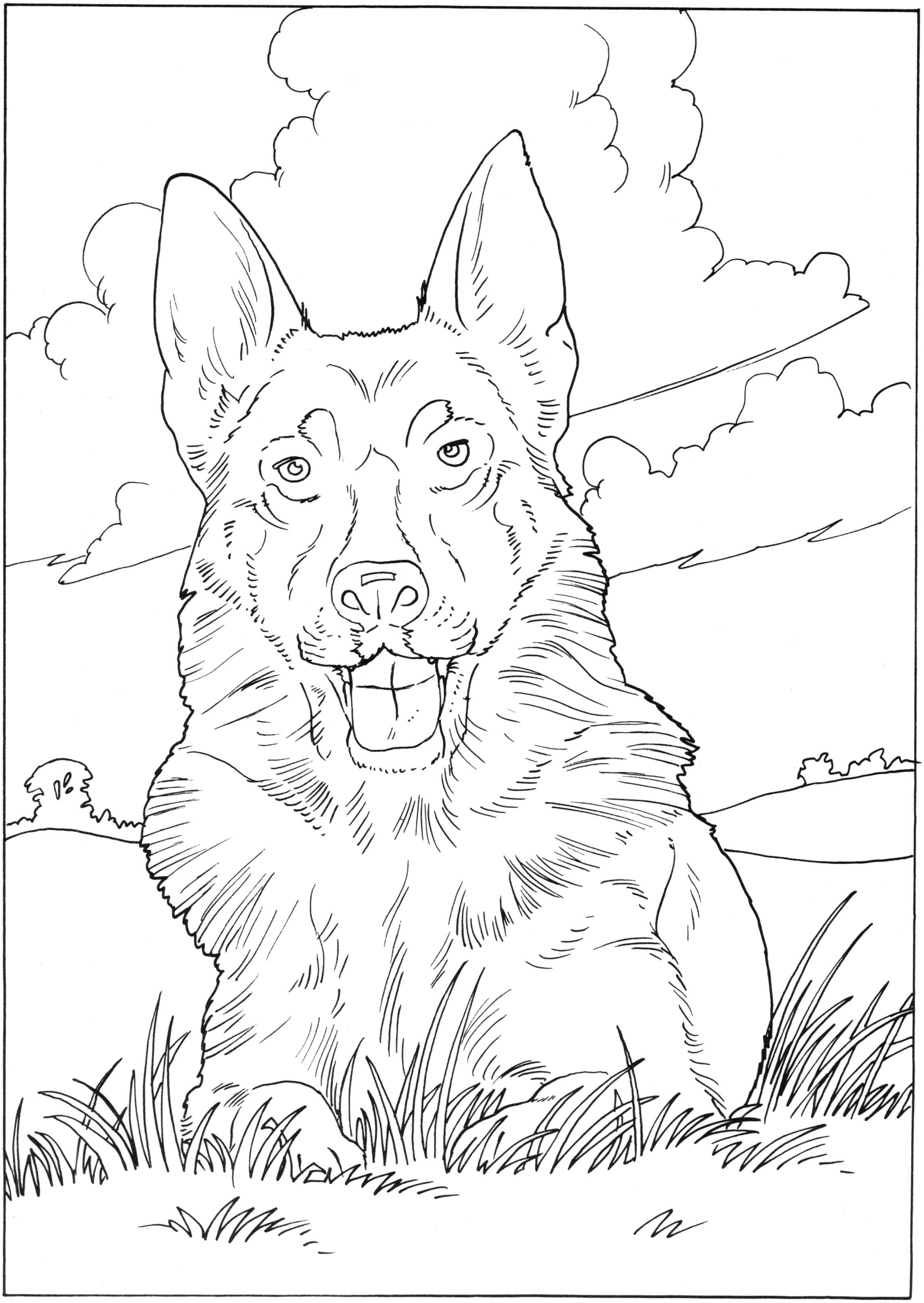

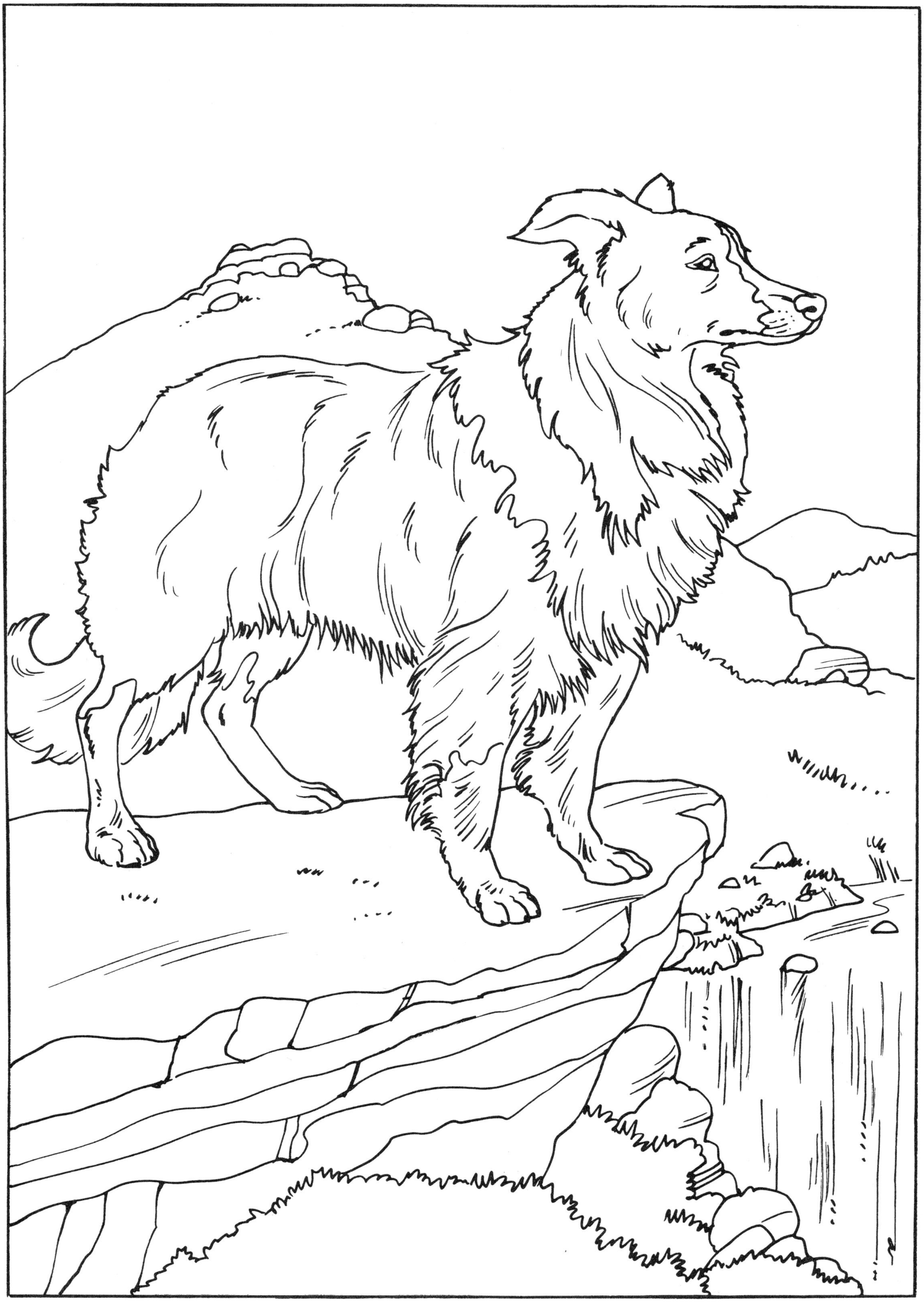

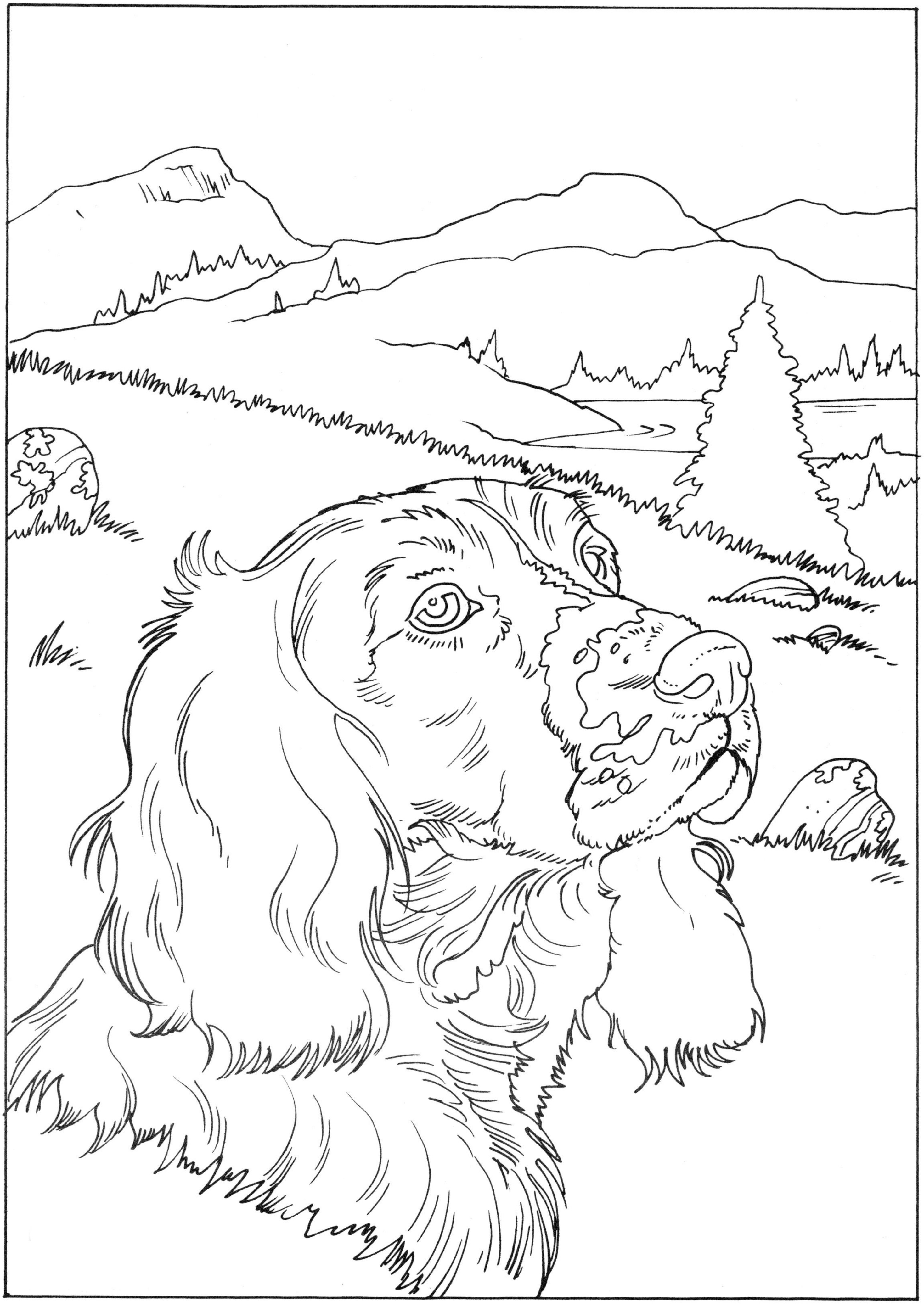

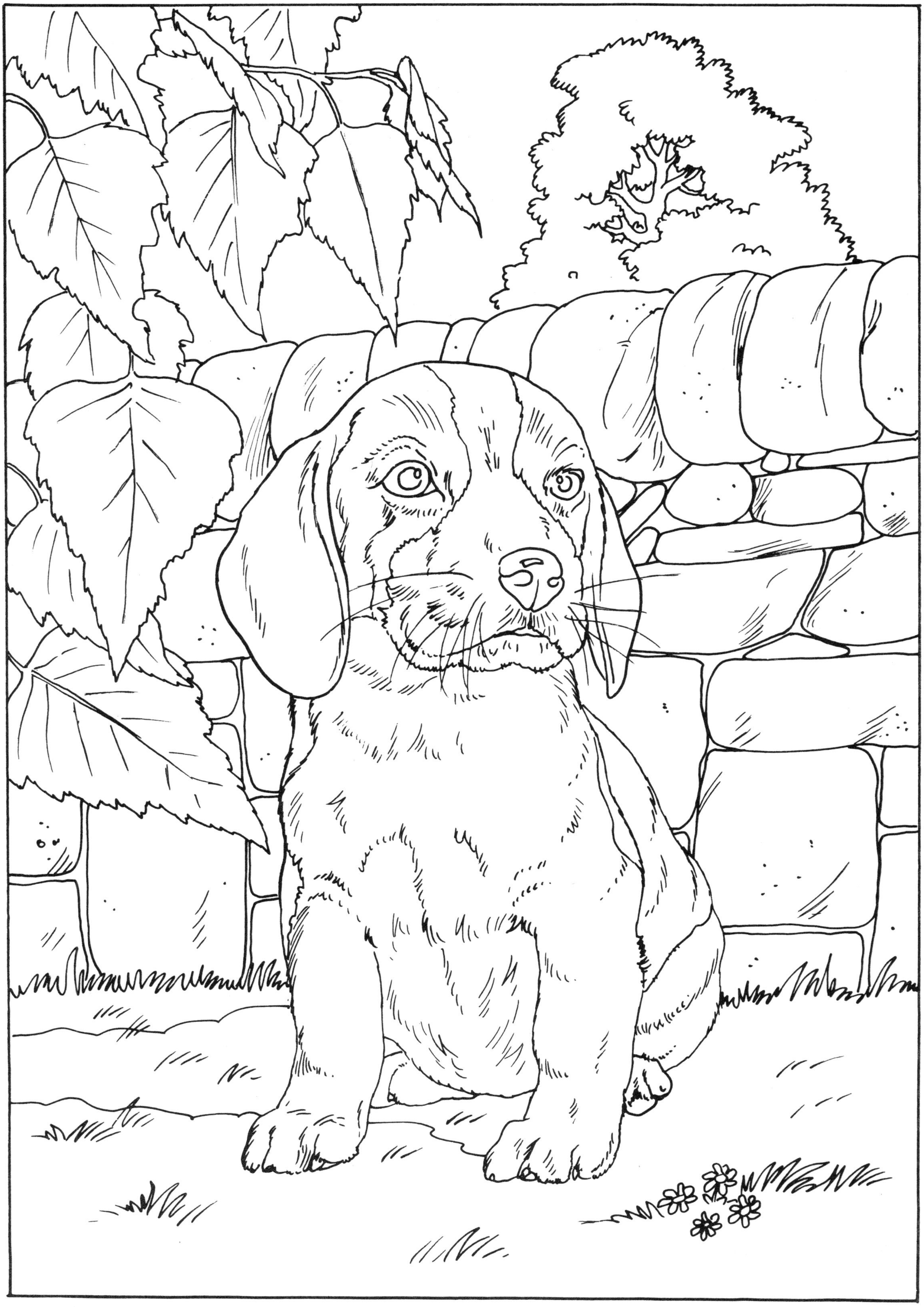

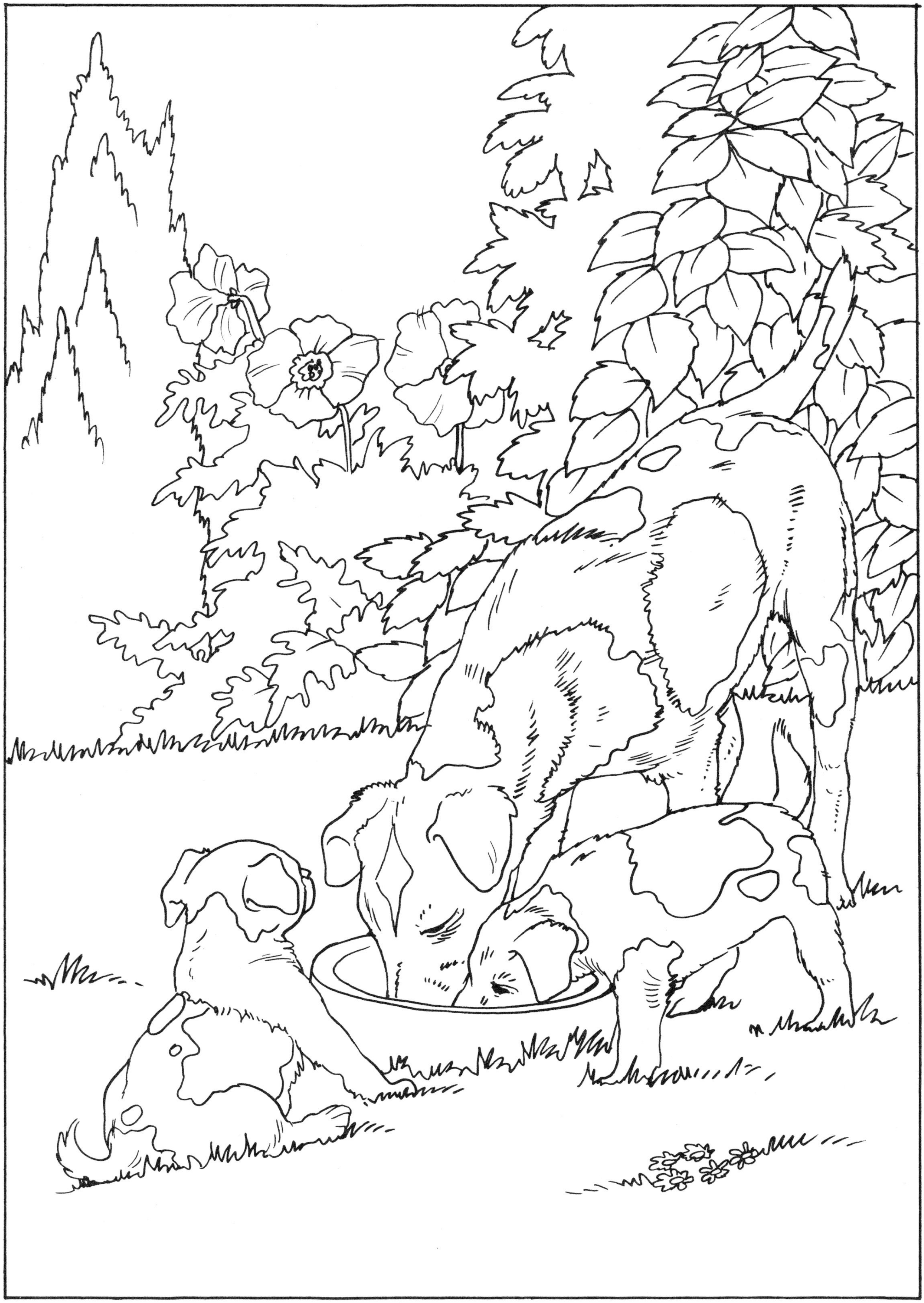

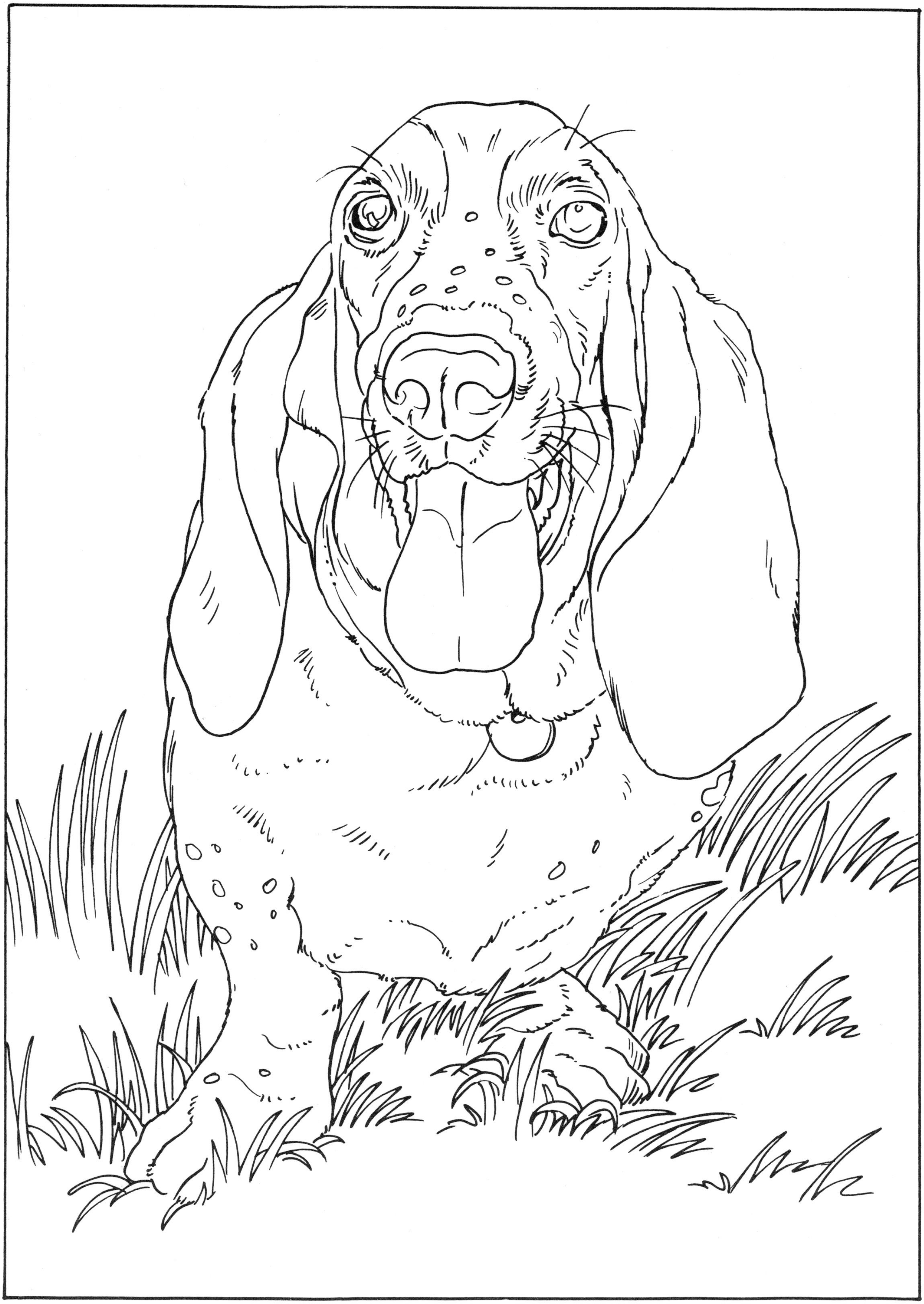

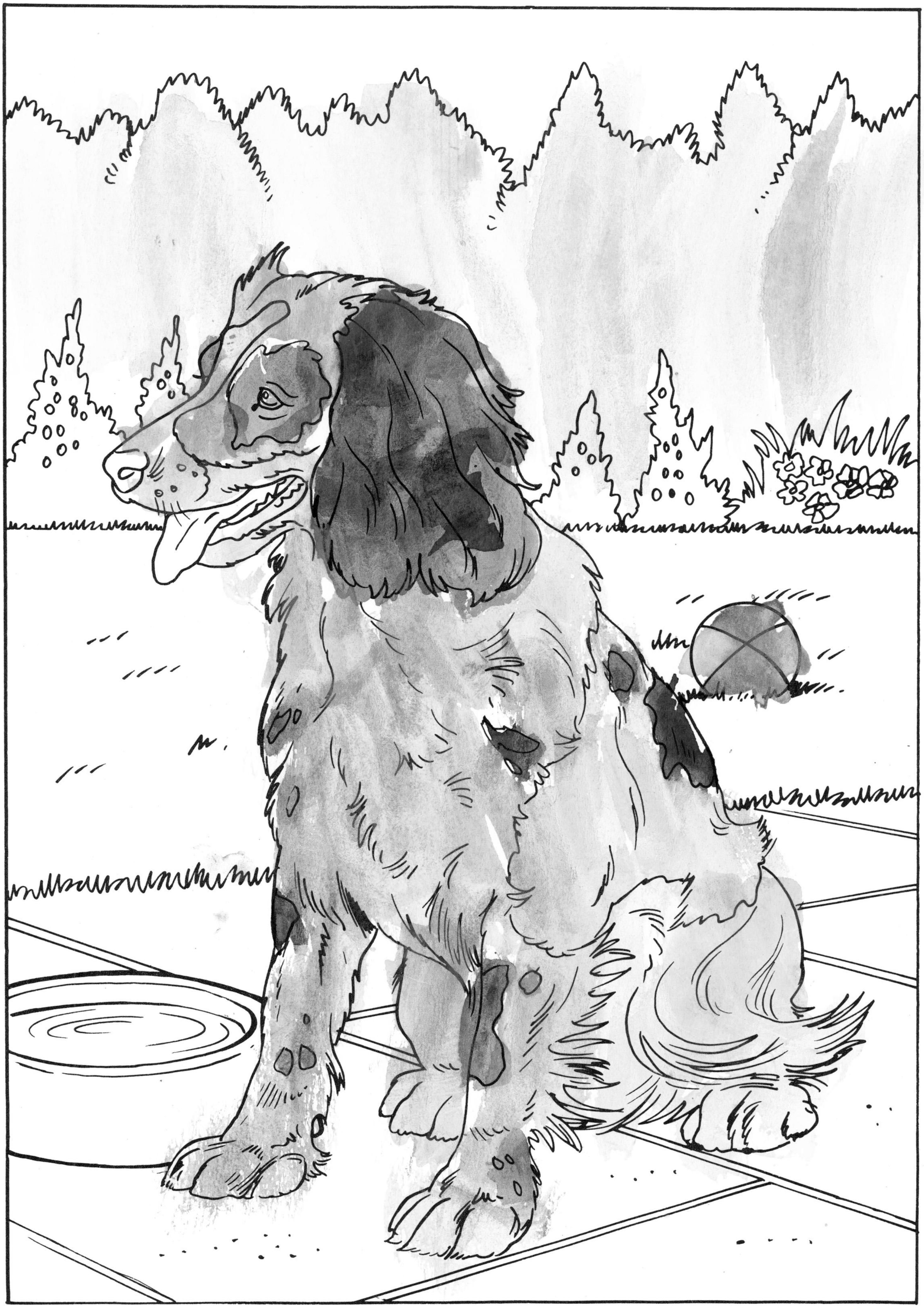

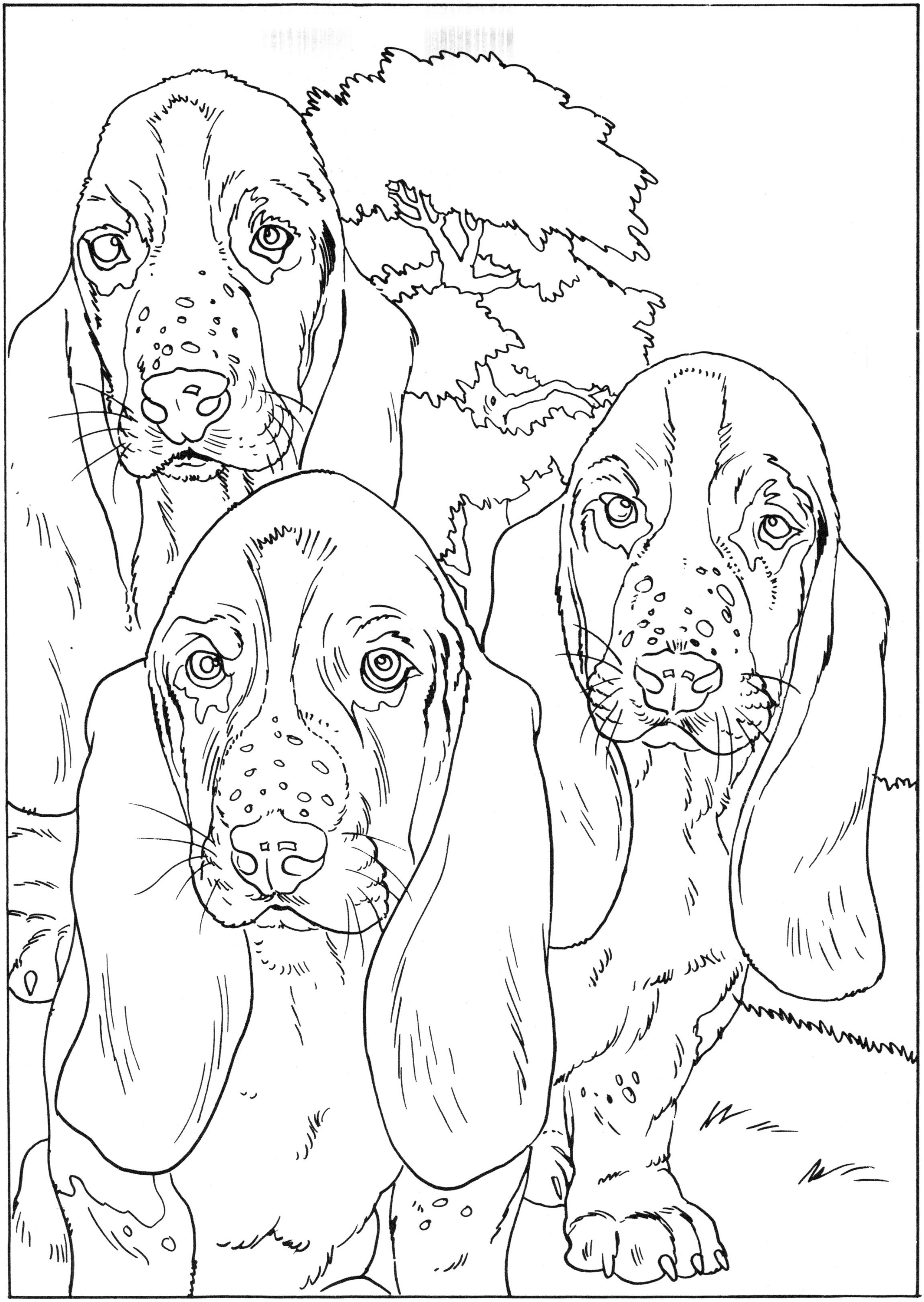

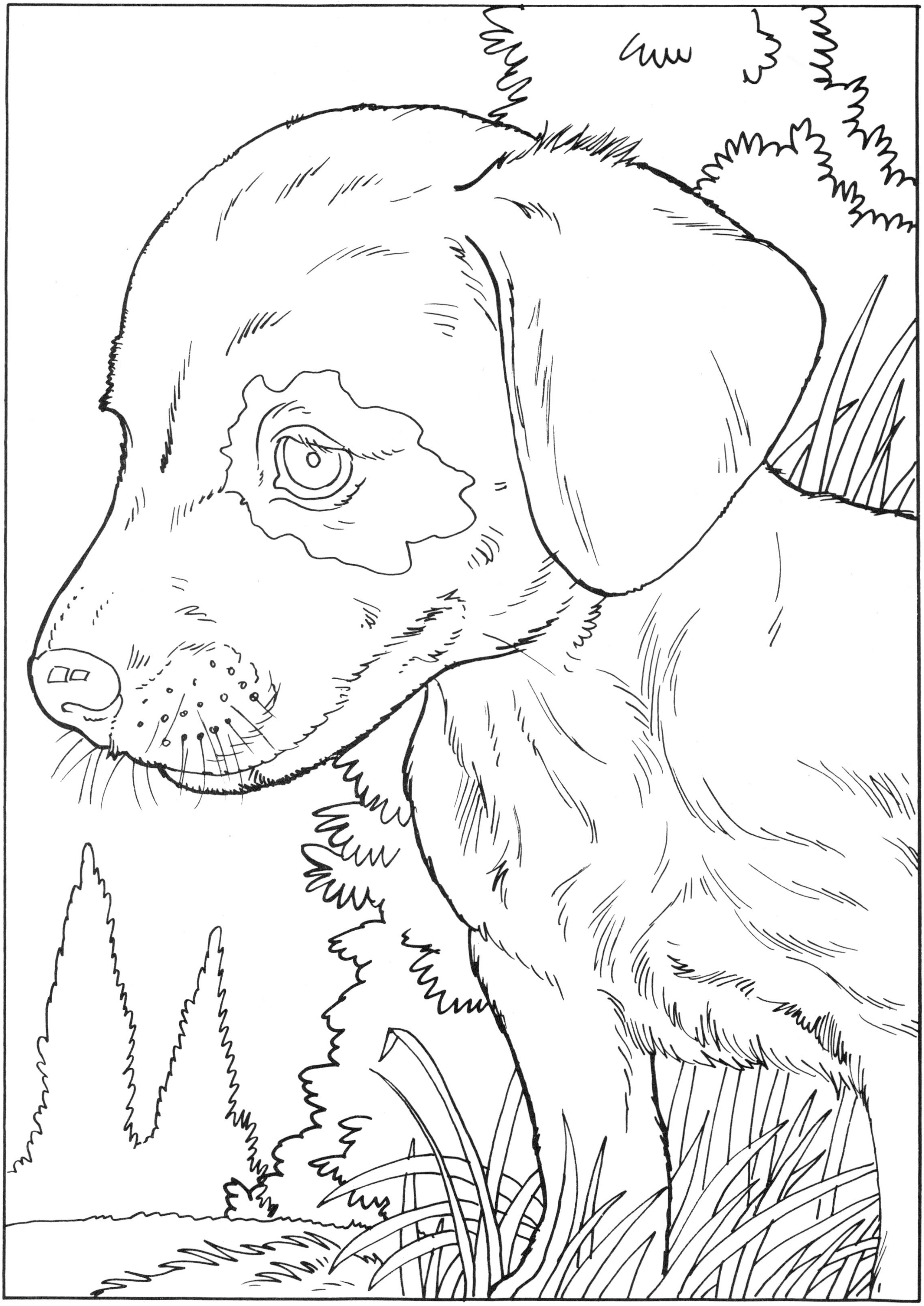

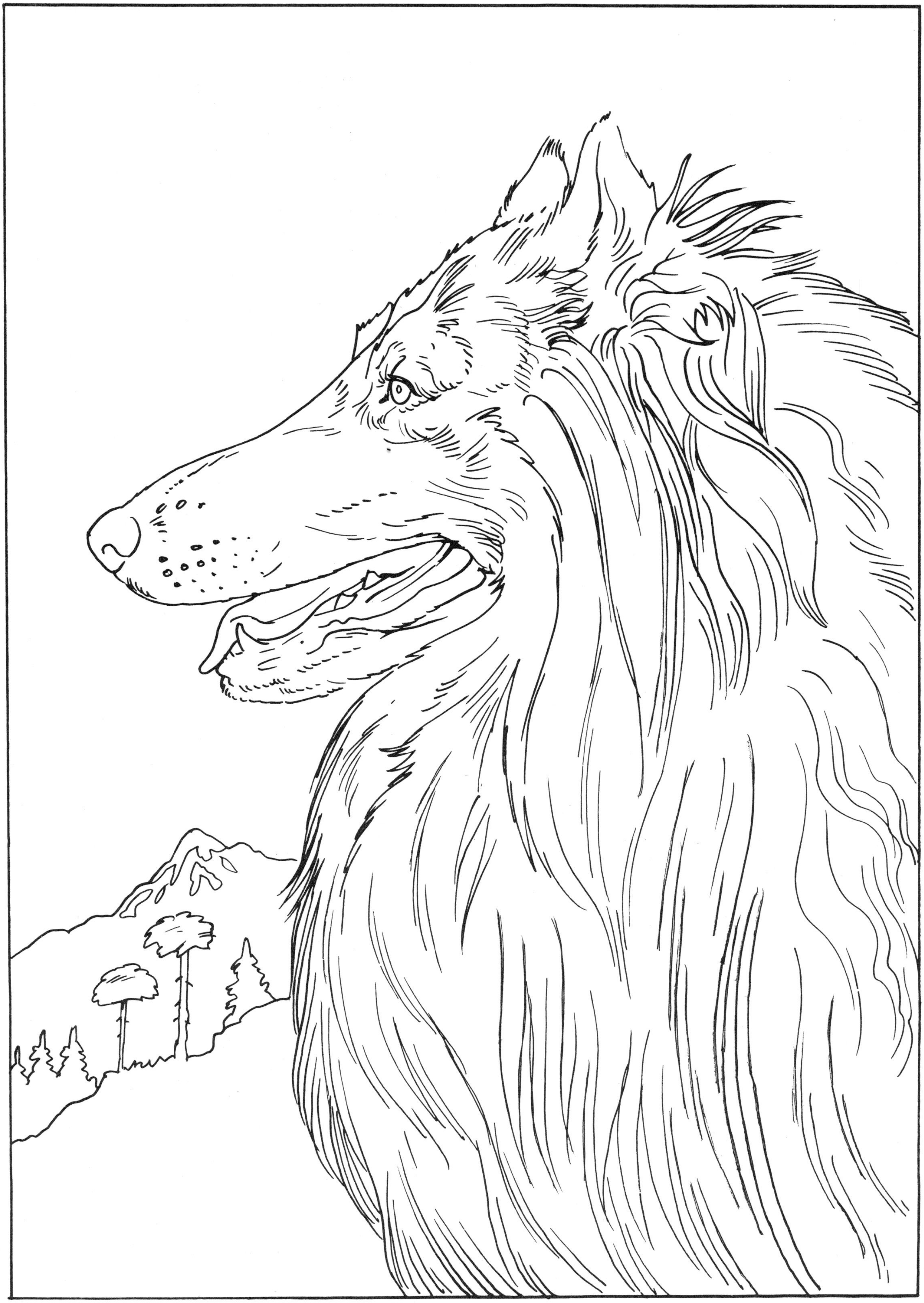

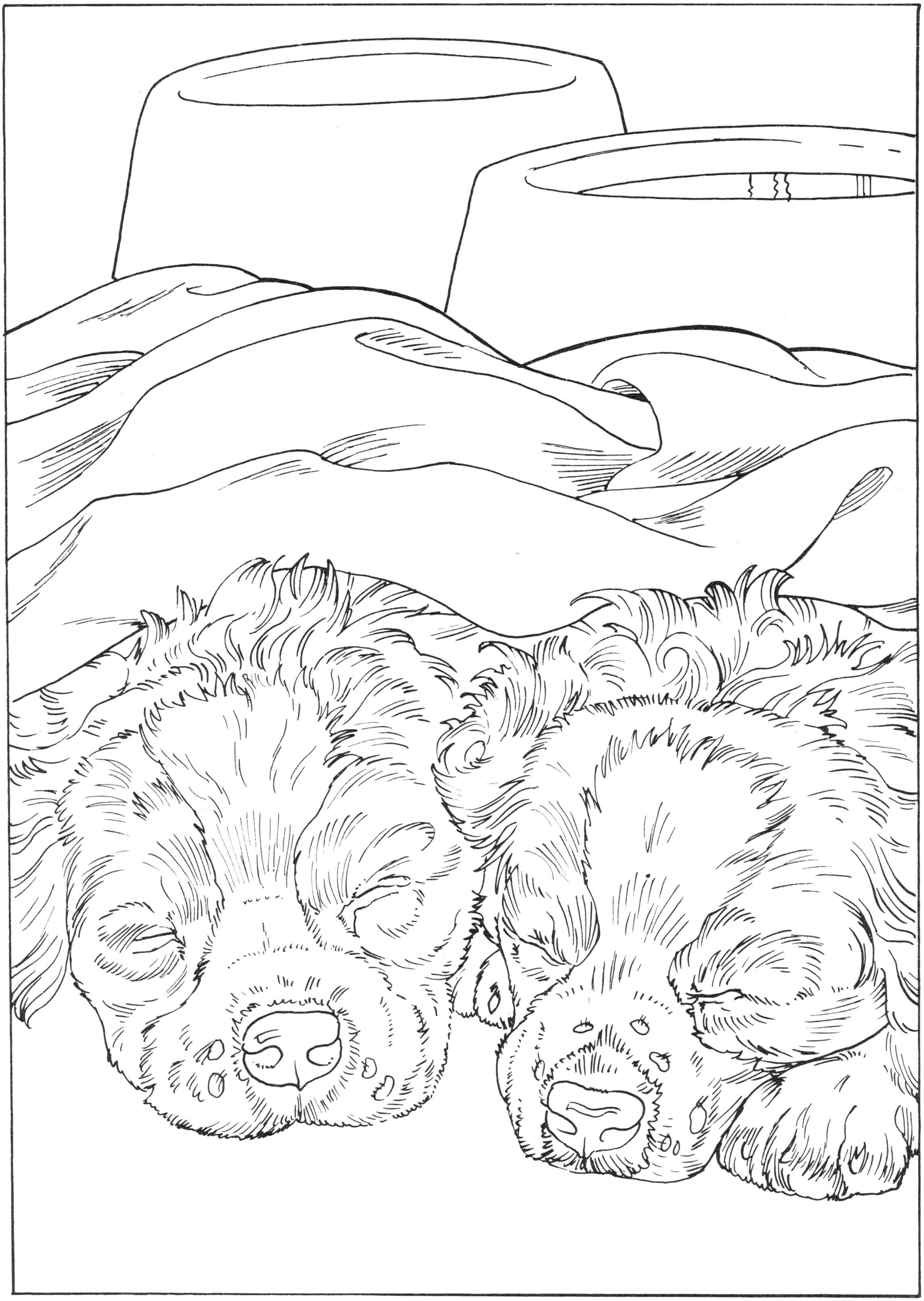

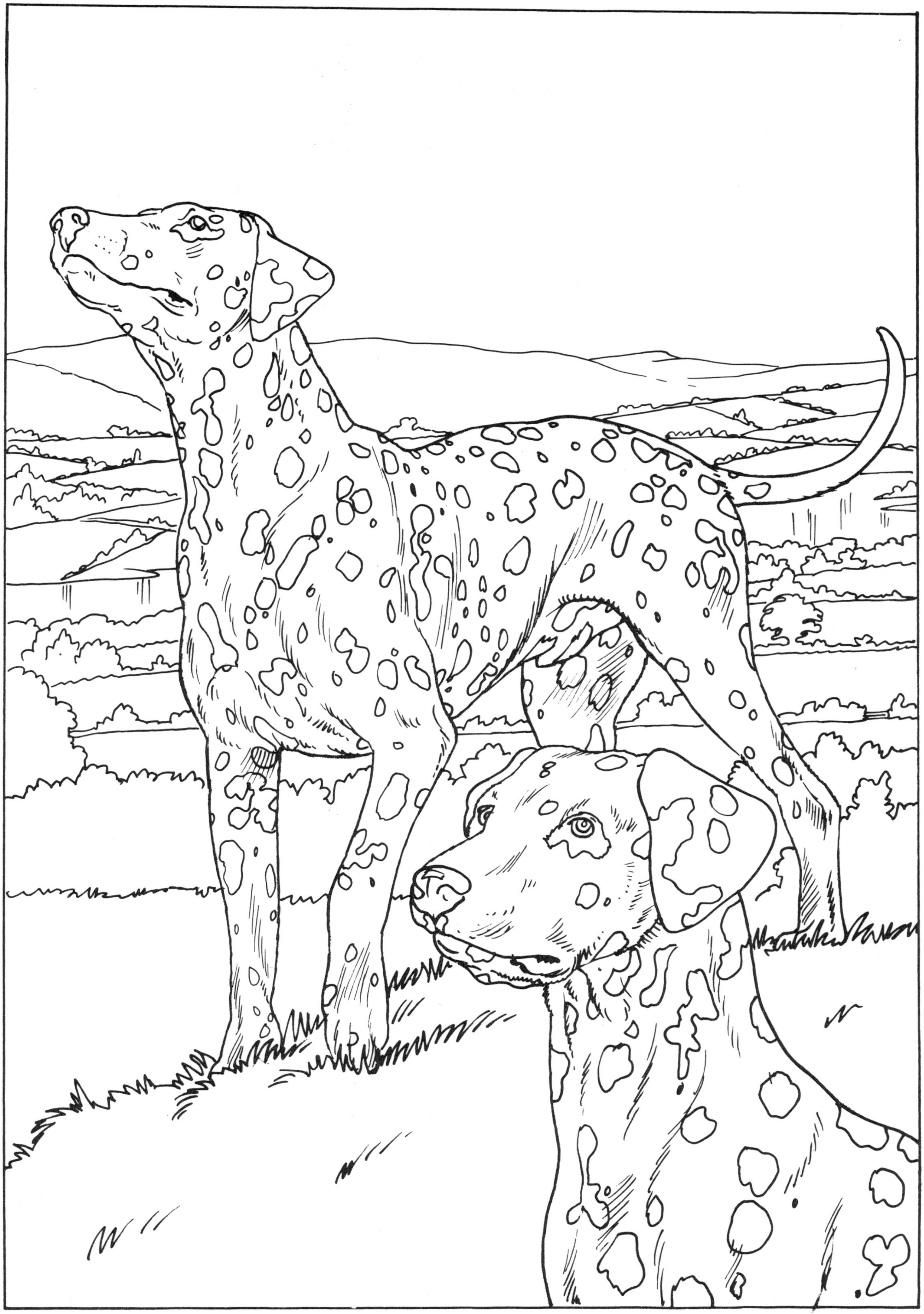

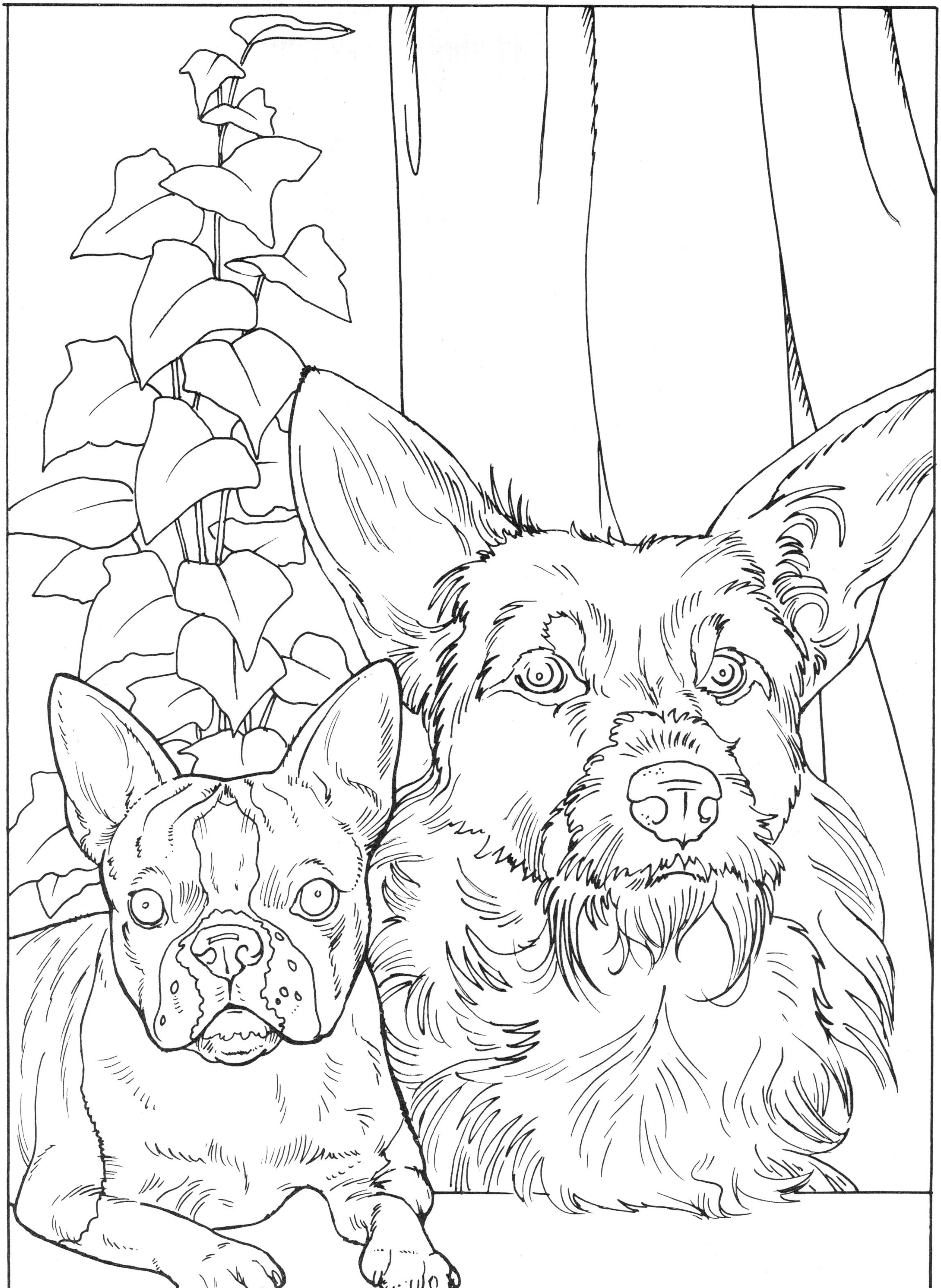

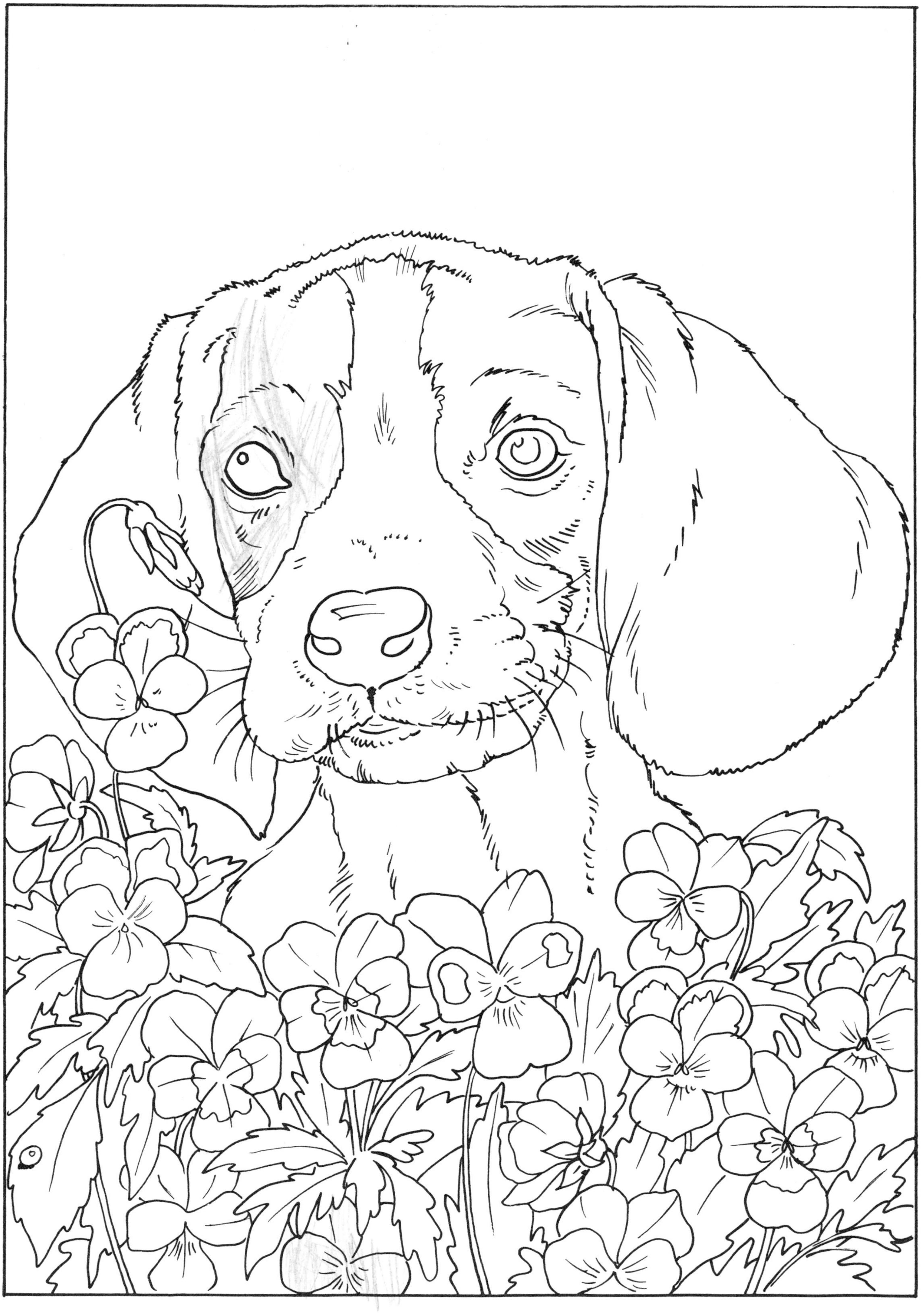

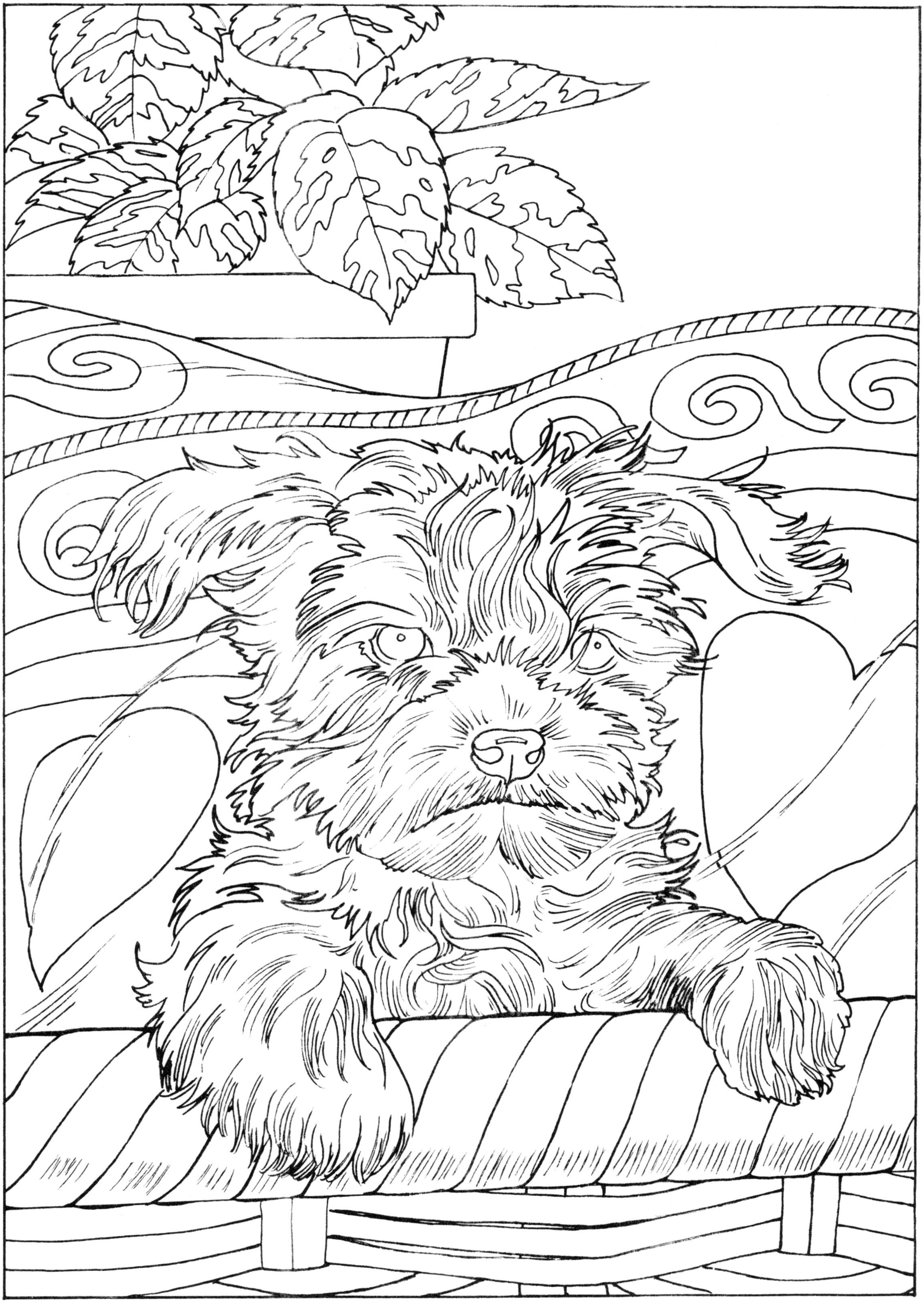

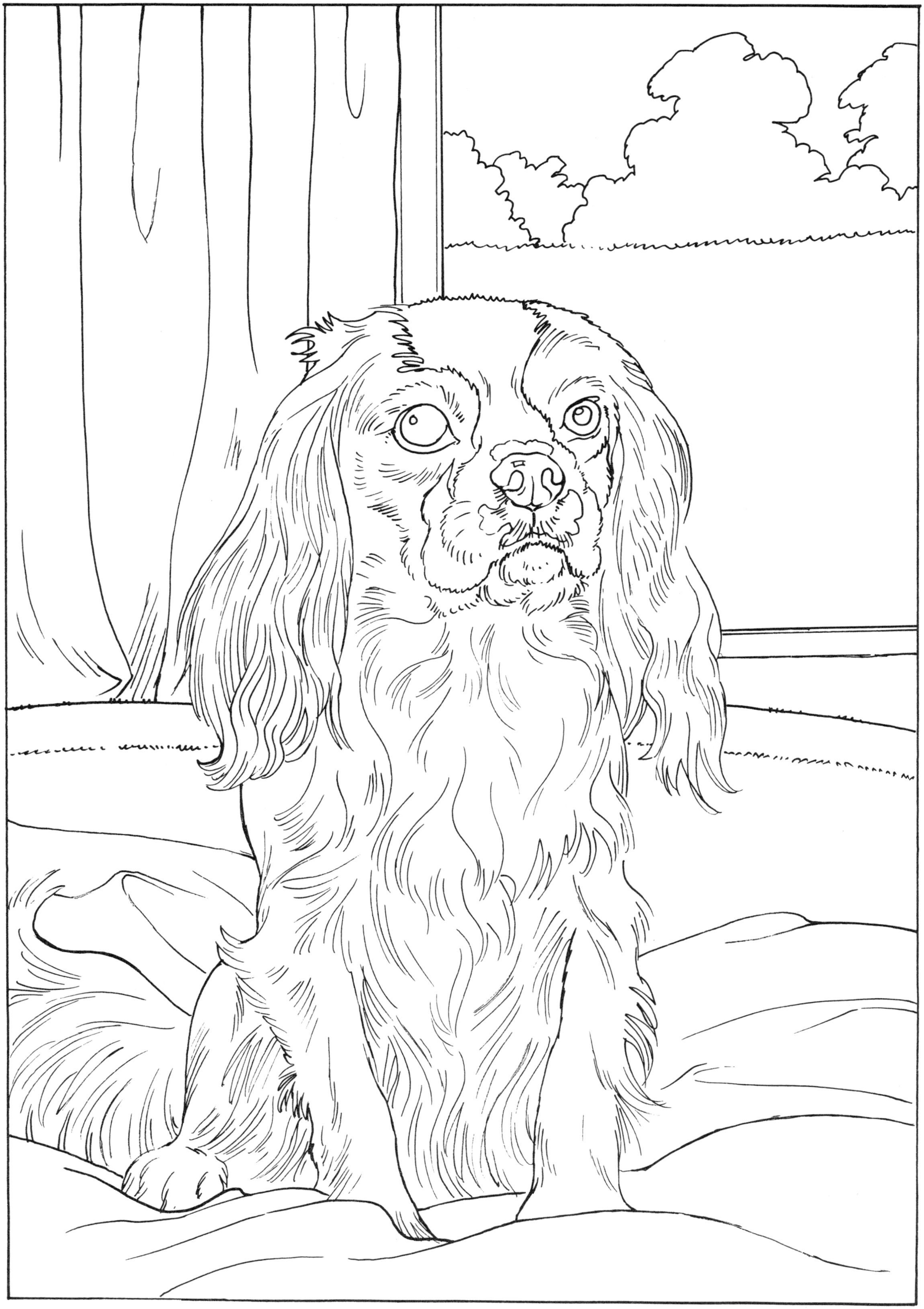

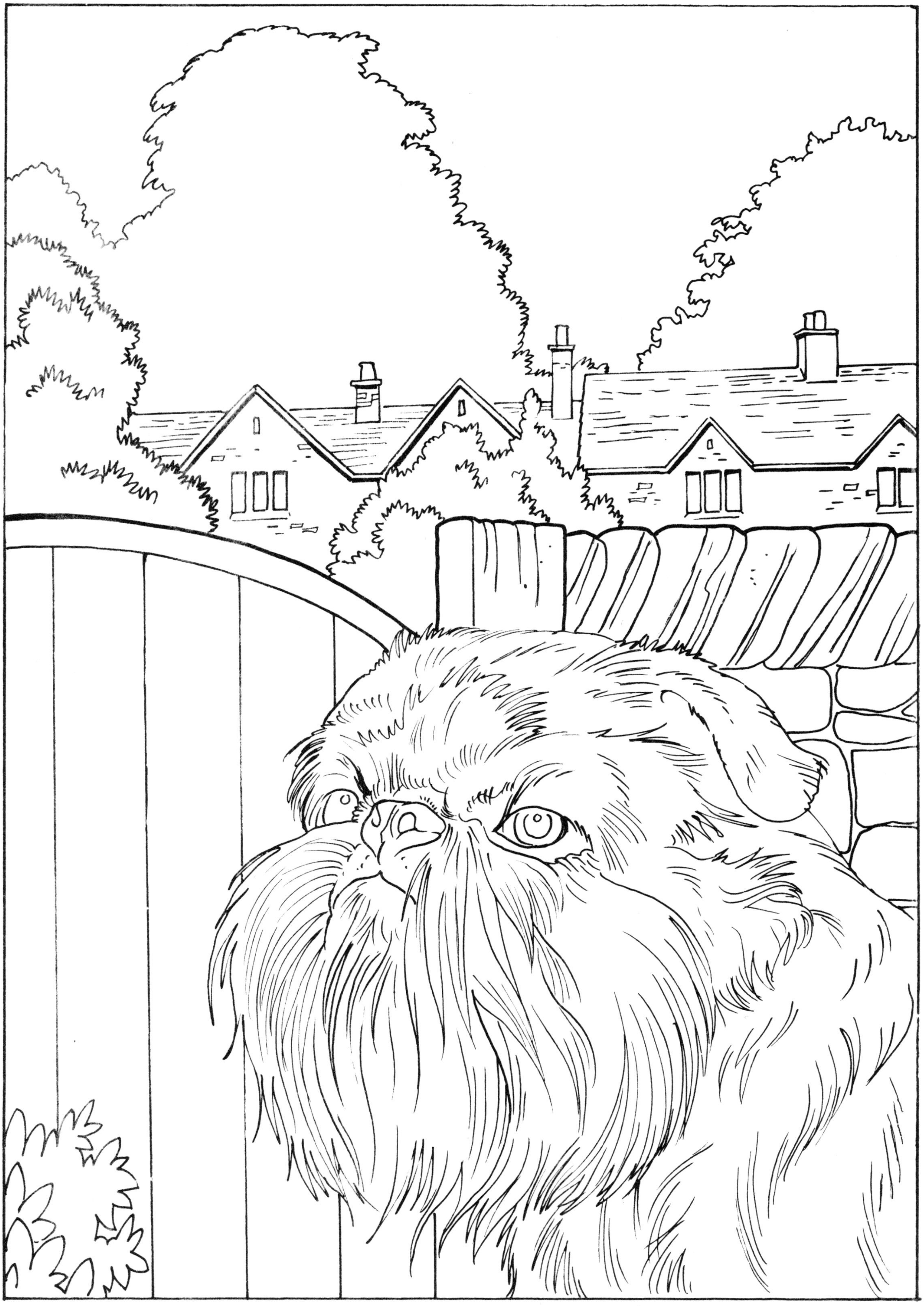

Published by Peter Haddock Publishing
United Kingdom.
Printed in India